W9-AUB-615

HERO JOURNALS

Shaka Zulu

Richard Spilsbury

Raintree

Chicago, Illinois

© 2014 Raintree
an imprint of Capstone Global Library, LLC
Chicago, Illinois

To contact Capstone Global Library, please
call 800-747-4992, or visit our web site
www.capstonepub.com

Edited by Adam Miller, Charlotte Guillain, and
Claire Throp
Designed by Richard Parker and Ken Vail Graphic
Design
Original illustrations © Capstone Global Library
Ltd 2014
Illustrated by Stathis Petropoulos
Picture research Tracy Cummins
Production by Victoria Fitzgerald
Originated by Capstone Global Library Ltd
Printed and bound in China by Leo Paper
Products Ltd

17 16 15 14 13
10 9 8 7 6 5 4 3 2 1

**Library of Congress Cataloging-in-Publication
Data**
Spilsbury, Richard, 1963-
    Shaka Zulu / Richard Spilsbury.
        p. cm.—(Hero journals)
    Includes bibliographical references and index.
    ISBN 978-1-4109-5361-2 (hb)—ISBN 978-1-4109-
5368-1 (pb) 1. Shaka, Zulu Chief, 1787?-1828—
Juvenile literature. 2. Zulu (African people)—Kings
and rulers—Biography—Juvenile literature. 3. Zulu
(African people)—History—19th century—Juvenile
literature. I. Title. II. Series: Hero journals.
    DT878.Z9S67 2014
    968.4—dc23   2012043532

Acknowledgments
We would like to thank the following for
permission to reproduce photographs: Alamy
pp. 23 (© FVE Media), 28 (© 19th era), 32 (© Mary
Evans Picture Library/Alamy); Bridgeman Art
Library pp. 4, 14, 22, 37, 38 (© Look and Learn), 6
(© The Stapleton Collection), 33 (© Ken Welsh),
35 (The Diary of Henry Francis Fynn after original
sketch by Henry Francis Fynn); Corbis pp. 5 (©
Mike Hutchings/Reuters), 9 (© Martin Harvey),
13 (© Selwyn Tait/Sygma); Getty Images pp. 11
(Ami Vitale), 16 (Daryl Balfour), 24-25 (Keystone
Features), 26 (Volkmar K. Wentzel/National
Geographic), 31 (Roger de la Harpe), 39 (Heinrich
van den Berg); Shutterstock pp. 27 bottom (©
Joe Mercier), 27 top (© Tim UR); Superstock pp.
17 (Bill Gozansky/age fotostock), 20 (Universal
Images Group).

Design elements supplied by Shutterstock (©
R-studio), (© Pavel K), (© Picsfive), (© karawan).

Cover photograph of Shaka Zulu restaurant statue
in Camden, London, England, reproduced with
permission of Alamy (© Tim Gainey).

Every effort has been made to contact copyright
holders of material reproduced in this book. Any
omissions will be rectified in subsequent printings
if notice is given to the publisher.

Contents

My Name Is Shaka Zulu

It is 1828, and very soon I will die. My people have had enough of me, even my brothers; they are coming now armed with spears. I am a very powerful man, and powerful men have enemies, I know that. It is true that I have killed many people and ordered the deaths of many more, some who did not deserve it. But blood had to spill to make the Zulu nation great and to show people that I am strong.

I have been thinking back with pride at my achievements. Can you imagine that I was born unwanted by my father and our people? That I learned how to fight and lead warriors in a huge Zulu army? Now my name is known throughout Africa and across seas. I am Shaka Zulu.

I am king of my people and a hero. People will remember me in the future.

The leader of the Zulu people in South Africa today is King Goodwill Zwelithini. Today's Zulus are part of an integrated South Africa. Zwelithini leads by promoting his people and their customs.

> *"Up! Children of Zulu, your day has come. Up! And destroy them all."*
> Shaka Zulu

Legacy

Shaka Zulu was a tyrant, but one of the greatest military leaders Africa has ever known. Through his leadership, Zulu power expanded from a clan living in an area of around 100 square miles (259 square kilometers) to a vast nation covering over 11,000 square miles (29,784 square kilometers). Today, there are around 10 million descendants of these Zulus in South Africa.

The Early Years

I was born in 1787 in southeastern Africa. I am the son of Senzangakona, king of the Zulu people. My mother's name is Nandi. She is the daughter of a chief of the Langeni people, who live nearby.

We live in a place called EmaKhosini, or Burial-Place of the Kings. You see, my Zulu ancestors have lived here for centuries. My people say that our first king was named Zulu. This means "Heaven." He came from farther north, where it was hot and dry. He settled at EmaKhosini because it was a green place with rivers. It is a good place to raise cattle and grow crops.

Our families lived in simple
huts made from grasses.

Our neighbors

The area ruled by my father Senzangakona—the Zulu chiefdom—is one of hundreds in these parts. Every chiefdom has a different chief and contains different clans. Our nearest neighbors are the Langeni people, and their chiefdom is bigger than ours. The older Zulus are always telling me and the other children not to stray too often onto the land of neighboring chiefdoms. We know this could lead to trouble and even deadly fighting.

People of southern Africa

Thousands of years ago, the southern African people were mostly small groups of hunter-gatherers. During the following centuries, different tribes who were cattle herders and farmers moved south from central Africa in search of land. One tribe called the Nguni settled in South Africa from around 300 BCE. The Zulu and Langeni chiefdoms were part of this tribe.

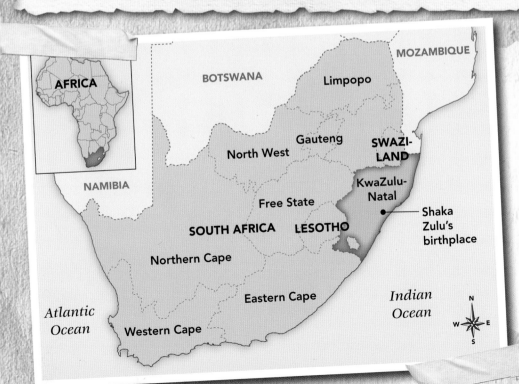

Shaka was born not far from the coast of present-day KwaZulu-Natal. This South African state is where most Zulus live today.

Rejected

Do you know how I got my name? I-Shaka means "the parasite"—an unwanted animal that lives and feeds inside someone. My people called me this to insult me. They did not think it was right that my mother gave birth without being married, and they did not want me in their clan.

I've lived in Senzangakona's kraal since my mother became his third wife months after my birth. But he ignores me. The other children tease me for being small and say I am not Senzangakona's son. I am rejected by my people.

Zulu settlements

A kraal is an enclosed settlement containing a central, fenced area for cattle and goats, surrounded by a circle of huts where family members live. The whole kraal is enclosed with a fence of sharpened stakes to keep out wild animals and enemy people who may want to kill or to steal livestock.

Leaving the Zulus

Today, we were banished from the Zulu kingdom. It is all my fault. I was looking after Senzangakona's sheep as they grazed. It was a hot day, and I accidentally dozed off. I woke to see a dog killing one of the sheep. Senzangakona was so angry with me that he told my mother to take me and my younger sister and go.

Like all Zulu children, I was expected to look after livestock while they grazed outside the kraal and also to tend to them inside.

Document it!

This book follows Shaka's life from birth to death. But journals don't have to be in order of dates. Your journal could be thematic with sections on different aspects of your life such as music, movies, fashion, or pets.

With the Langeni

We are now back living among my mother's people, the Langeni. It took one day to walk to their home in the Mhlathuze Valley, around 20 miles (30 kilometers) away. I remember thinking that things would get better for us, but they have gotten even worse. The Langeni boys are worse than the Zulus. They bully me and tell me I do not belong with them. The only friendly faces I have seen since arriving are my two Zulu aunts who visit often. They are my father's other two wives and always got along well with my mother.

> *"Never mind, my Um-lilwane [Little Fire], you have got the isibindi [courage] of a lion and one day you will be the greatest chief in the land."*
>
> Nandi, spoken to Shaka

Drought

It is 1802, and we are on the move again. This time it is because of Madlantule, or drought. There have been so many hot months with no rain. Many Langeni cattle have died and people are starving, so we've been sent away. We will go north to stay with my mother's aunt in the Mthethwa chiefdom. Maybe life will be better there.

The grass has turned
brown all around and the
maize is too dry and hard
to eat.

Maize

Southern African people started to grow maize
(corn) to eat in the 18th century after meeting
Portuguese farmers growing it in what is now
Mozambique. Maize produces lots of filling food
on small areas of land and can be dried easily
for storage. But it needs lots of water to grow.

Standing out

At last, I am happy! I like living among the Mthethwa. At first, I still got bullied, but not anymore. Why? Because I have grown tall and strong and have discovered that I am very good at Zulu stick fighting. No other teenager of my age can beat me in a match! Finally, the other boys have started to respect me. They follow me in games and we hunt for wild animals such as leopards. I can't wait until I am old enough to become a Mthethwa soldier. Then I will prove my fighting skills among men.

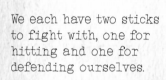

We each have two sticks to fight with, one for hitting and one for defending ourselves.

In the army

The other soldiers call me Nodumehlezi. It means "the one who causes the earth to rumble," by making the enemy run away and by leading my soldiers into war. I was 23 when I joined the army and was soon noticed by the Mthethwa chief, Dingiswayo. He saw that I was brave and could lead others. Now, six years later, I am a top commander of his troops.

These modern Zulu men are taking part in a dance festival. With their spears and shields, it is not difficult to imagine how fearsome Zulu warriors must have been.

Dingiswayo

Dingiswayo was leader of the Mthethwa chiefdom, which was made up of several small, independent clans. He created a trained, professional army after learning about how European armies were run. The success of the Mthethwa in battle influenced how other African armies were organized.

Zulu Leader

I am now leader of the Zulus! It started with my father Senzangakona's death. I know he did not like me, but I am his eldest son and therefore the rightful heir to the Zulu chiefdom. He must have heard about my leadership skills, but still he chose my brother Sigujana as his successor. Knowing how I felt, Dingiswayo lent me soldiers to challenge Sigujana and his loyal troops for the leadership of the Zulus. There was no other way but to kill Sigujana. Now his troops and all Zulus follow me.

Here I am about to lead my men in battle.

New weapons

We are an army of 400, but not yet the fighting force I want. I have seen in battle how enemies are killed when stabbed with short spears close up, but are more often only injured when hit by long spears thrown from a distance. So I have asked a good blacksmith in a neighboring clan to make short spears from strong metal with broad, sharp blades. With these new weapons, my soldiers will be invincible.

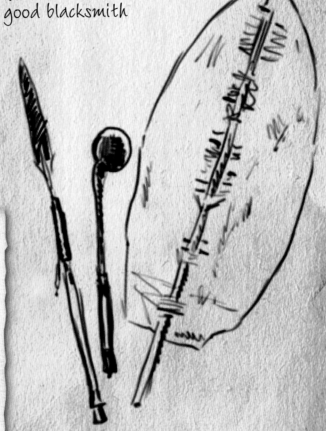

Guns

Zulus mostly fought in close combat using spears in the 18th and 19th centuries, and they rarely used guns. Any guns they had were often those seized in battle from other clans. These other clans sometimes traded goods such as animal skins, fresh food, and water for guns from Europeans living in coastal settlements such as Cape Colony (an area around present-day Cape Town).

"Shaka called the new stabbing spear iKlwa after the sucking sound it supposedly made when it was withdrawn from the victim's flesh."

Bruce Vandervort, author of a book on wars in Africa, 1998

New organization

Dingiswayo taught me how to organize an army. I have divided the soldiers up by age and fighting experience into regiments called amabutho. Each amabutho lives in a separate kraal with its own herd of cattle of different skin color than the others. People can tell which amabutho a man comes from by the distinctive hide shields, headdresses, and ornaments. Soldiers in an amabutho are like brothers and would die for each other in battle.

There can be no finer cattle in the world than our Zulu animals, descendants of the great Nguni cattle of our ancestors.

Cattle

Cattle were very important for Zulus and other clans in southern Africa. They provided meat, milk, leather, horn for ornaments and containers, and dung for fuel. They were also a sign of wealth. Rich, important people had large herds, and clans took herds from other clans they defeated as a sign of military success.

Army life

My amabuthos must train as hard as I did so they are fit and mobile. The soldiers are slow at first, but they soon think nothing of marching 50 miles (80 kilometers) a day. Amabuthos can only leave the army when I decide they have given their all—usually when they are past 40 years old. Then I decorate them with a special headring, give them cattle, and allow them to marry.

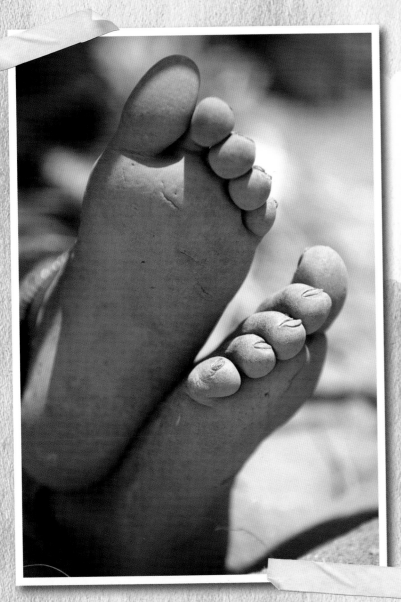

My feet are like leather and I can run over thorny ground for many miles. I expect my troops to do the same.

Document it!

Shaka enjoyed being part of a team. Keep a record of what you did with any clubs or other groups and record who was on your teams. Newspaper clippings and photos are fascinating and will help you remember in the future.

Fighting

A Zulu soldier must be fit, brave, and willing to fight to the death for me and for his amabutho. But we can only win battles if the amabuthos are well organized and fight together. So I have taught them the "bull's horns strategy" that I learned in the Mthethwe army. The fighting force divides up into four groups who attack, surround, and then destroy the enemy.

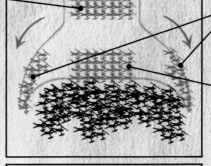

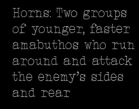

Horns: Two groups of younger, faster amabuthos who run around and attack the enemy's sides and rear

Loins: A group that sits and waits to reinforce our numbers if too many fall

Chest: My most experienced amabuthos who charge and fight the enemy head-on

It is a beautiful sight to see my army swarm like biting ants around a fallen locust.

In the heat of battle, I cannot be everywhere to tell all my amabuthos what to do. So I rely on my trusted friend Ngomane and other indunas (officers) to help organize the Zulu forces. The indunas use hand signals to communicate with the soldiers—for example, to tell them where to go. They also keep in constant touch with the soldiers not actually in battle, including my youngest troops, to tell them to bring more weapons or food for the fighting amabuthos.

> "Strike an enemy once and for all.
> Let him cease to exist as a tribe or he
> will live to fly in your throat again."
>
> Shaka Zulu, from *Shaka Zulu: The Rise of the Zulu Empire* (1955) by E. A. Ritter

Ngomane

Ngomane was a trusted induna of Dingiswayo and leader of the Mthethwa chiefdom. He became friends with Shaka and Nandi when they first moved away from the Langeni clan. They were so close that he helped Shaka become chief of the Zulus and stayed with him as second-in-command.

My Kingdom Grows

Now is the time to make my Zulu kingdom bigger. We need more grazing land for our cattle and more soldiers for our army. We have started attacking neighboring clans.

My soldiers love to wash their spears in the blood of our enemies.

Revenge

Last week, I finally took revenge against the Langeni clan, who had so mistreated my mother and me when I was a boy. We marched at night and surrounded the kraal of the Langeni chief. He surrendered, and I had no argument with him. But when we left later the same day, those who had made our lives miserable were dead or dying, and the surviving Langeni had become part of the Zulu chiefdom.

> "The slayers will sharpen the...poles in this cattle-kraal—one for each of you. They will then...impale you on each of the sharpened poles. There you will stay till you die, and your bodies, or what will be left of them by the birds, will stay there as a testimony to all, what punishment awaits those who slander [mistreat] me and my mother."

Shaka Zulu warning the Langeni of his revenge, from *Shaka Zulu: The Rise of the Zulu Empire* (1955) by E. A. Ritter

Document it!

Many quotes by Shaka come from a book written by a man named Erneste Ritter. Ritter had heard the stories of Shaka partly from his Zulu servant, whose father had been one of Shaka's soldiers. The stories were passed down from father to son. Some remembered stories about events in your family may not be completely accurate, but they are still important records of past events.

Battling the Ndwandwe

It is 1818, and my kingdom has suddenly grown bigger. My friend and teacher Dingiswayo was murdered by Zwide, chief of the Ndwandwe clan. As his most trusted commander, I took over Dingiswayo's Mthethwe chiefdom and took his army into my Zulu kingdom. We have vowed to smash the Ndwandwe and avenge Dingiswayo's death, even though they have a bigger army.

We will not rest until the earth is soaked in Ndwandwe blood!

Zwide

Zwide was chief of the Ndwandwe from 1805 to 1825. The Ndwandwe attacked the Mthethwe people for years, partly hoping to capture them as slaves for sale to Portuguese traders living on the coast in the north. The traders wanted African slaves to work on sugar plantations in Brazil, where they had a colony.

Gqokli Hill

My heart races at the thought of the Battle of Gqokli Hill. The Zulu army tricked the Ndwandwe into thinking we had a much larger force attacking from one direction by using many decoy oxen and carts without people in them. Then we attacked them from another direction. Zwide was defeated, and now the Ndwandwe people are ruled by the Zulus, too!

Gqokli Hill overlooks the White Umfolozi River.

"Great nation of Zulu, You have shown courage against a superior enemy. The nations that spoke of you with contempt are chilled by your songs. Kings and princes shiver in their little thrones. Enemies flee to hide in the mountain caves."

Shaka, after beating the Ndwandwe

My capital

I have named my capital city *KwaBulawayo*, which means "at the place of suffering." This name reminds me of my childhood and how my life has changed. *KwaBulawayo* is a mighty, royal kraal of 1,400 circular huts made from good sticks and grasses. Each has a hard floor of cattle dung and soil. We have many grain pits, because whenever I defeat another clan my soldiers seize supplies of maize and millet grain to help feed my people.

isiZulu

isiZulu is the Zulu language. It is a mixture of the Xhosa language, used originally in southern Africa, and the language used by Nguni people who moved into the area. One way Shaka controlled his kingdom was to make everyone use the same mix of words in one Zulu language. Today, isiZulu is still spoken by around 10 million people. See the "Find Out More" section in this book for a web site where you can learn isiZulu words.

Document it!

Write about and take photos of where you live for your journal. Your house, street, or town may seem too familiar now, but in the future these records will bring back all sorts of memories.

The royal kraal would have looked a
little like this one in Lesotho.

Zulu women

Zulu women in my kingdom manage their households, while the men take care of the fighting. I also need women in my life. My Zulu aunts understand why I would choose one plan and not another. So they are the ones who make decisions when I am away. They also make sure soldiers of one clan only marry women of another. You see, clans with mixed blood will not rise up against me.

I cannot understand why other leaders have sons. Dingiswayo was a great leader, but when he was young, he plotted with his brother to take over the Mthethwe from his father. I don't want to be looking over my shoulder for trouble, so I will not get married and I will not have children.

This modern-day Zulu princess is playing an instrument called an ugubhu.

State cattle

I never tire of looking at the cattle in our Royal Herds. There are so many partly because my aunts took the most desirable young women from important Zulu clans and offered them as brides to wealthy men in other Zulu clans. The men had to give many cattle to the Royal Herds to pay me for the right to marry.

Wealth in Africa

Cattle were a sign of wealth for Zulus, but Europeans were attracted to Africa for other valuable resources. These included slaves to work in mines and on plantations growing sugarcane in the Americas. The Portuguese first took African slaves in the 15th century. Other valuable African resources in Shaka's time included elephant ivory, copper, and spices such as pepper.

pepper

elephant tusks

27

The Crushing

The land is not so good now, so my forces need to spread further to get what we need. Other tribes fear the brutal power of my army. We take young women and men to live with us. But we slaughter older people, since they are no use to us. Some tribes, such as the Ndebele, have fled, leaving empty lands. We call this Mfecane—"the crushing."

Mzilikazi

Mzilikazi was a trusted induna of Shaka, but also a leader of the Ndebele tribe. In 1822, Shaka sent Mzilikazi and his troops to fight a tribe on his behalf. Mzilikazi won, but he refused to hand over the spoils of battle to Shaka because he wanted power. He led the Ndebele tribe north, crushing other tribes on the way. After seven years, they settled in an area called Matabeleland, part of present-day Zimbabwe.

The Ndebele were also known as the Matabele people.

New kingdoms

I hear that the Ngwane, Sotho, and Kololo tribes went over the Drakensberg Mountains to the west. The Ndebele are traveling up the Vaal riverbanks in search of somewhere to build permanent kraals. These new kingdoms may one day grow big, but they will never match the Zulus!

Outside pressures

Some historians believe that Shaka's desire for a bigger kingdom was just one reason for the movement of tribes during the Mfecane. Another reason may have been the presence of slave traders in southern Africa that forced clans to move for safety. Tribes may also have moved to look for better maize farmland due to drought.

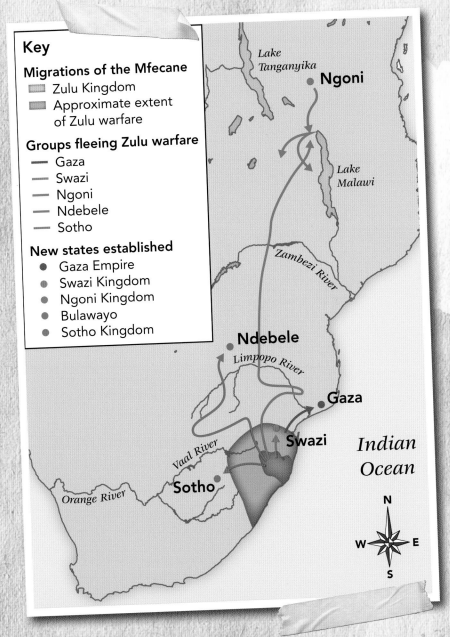

Key

Migrations of the Mfecane
- Zulu Kingdom
- Approximate extent of Zulu warfare

Groups fleeing Zulu warfare
— Gaza
— Swazi
— Ngoni
— Ndebele
— Sotho

New states established
● Gaza Empire
● Swazi Kingdom
● Ngoni Kingdom
● Bulawayo
● Sotho Kingdom

Lake Tanganyika

Ngoni

Lake Malawi

Zambezi River

Ndebele

Limpopo River

Gaza

Swazi

Indian Ocean

Vaal River

Sotho

Orange River

N W E S

The Mfecane during the 1820s led to several new states and empires forming in southern Africa outside the Zulu kingdom.

Wasteland

Huts are burning and fields lie untended. Hyenas and vultures feed on hundreds of dead bodies. This is what my indunas have told me they have seen again and again in the lands around my kingdom. They have even seen people so hungry that they would eat other people to stay alive. This has happened because tribes scattered by Zulu advances have destroyed villages they have moved through in search of new places to live.

I did not intend to create this wasteland in return for a greater Zulu kingdom.

Unrest

I can feel growing unrest in the Zulu kingdom. There are rumors that some members of my family want a new leader for the Zulu people. They think that the endless battles for new lands are weakening the kingdom. It is not surprising that people whose tribes were pushed from their lands, and forced to go hungry by my troops, have a grudge against me. This includes tribes like the Qwabe, who have fled but who once helped me in battle against Zwide and upon whose ancestral lands I built KwaBulawayo.

When tribes moved on, they took as many cattle as they could, to start a new life elsewhere.

Document it!

In Shaka's time, wars between tribes were common. When you create your journal, include some information about any wars, conflicts, or political events of the time. This puts the details of your life and times into an historical context.

Changing Kingdom

Some weeks ago, a messenger arrived at Kwa Bulawayo saying a great ship called *Antelope* had arrived at Port Natal nearby. The white men aboard wanted to meet me. I kept them waiting for a few weeks. But finally, I invited them to my kraal. They arrived on horseback carrying gifts, including new guns, and then they ate with me. One man, Henry Fynn, spoke our isiZulu language. He told me about the powerful English king and their hopes for setting up a trading station at Port Natal.

The leader of the men who landed in 1824 was Francis Farewell. He knew the importance of good relations with Shaka in setting up an English settlement.

"I hear you have come from umGeorge [King George], is it so? Is he as great a king as I am?"

Shaka to Henry Fynn

My gift of land began a change in my area. Hundreds of English people moved into the Zulu kingdom.

Gift

Henry Fynn is very interested in our Zulu life and has been staying at my kraal. This is a good thing, because his medicines saved my life after I was stabbed at a crowded dance by one of Zwide's men. In thanks, I gave him a gift of land around Port Natal. The British said that since Henry Fynn was one of them, that meant the land was owned by King George. So they have their trading station!

British in South Africa

In 1806, the British were fighting the French army, which was led by Napoleon. They took over Cape Colony from Dutch colonists there to stop Napoleon from controlling trade routes to Asia. In 1820, around 4,000 poor British settlers immigrated to live and help defend the Cape from local tribes. Some of the settlers moved to Port Natal—present-day Durban—in May 1824.

Dukuza

We have just finished building a large, new barracks near Port Natal at Dukuza. Seeing my fine Zulu troops every day will remind the British of my power. We can also keep an eye on what they are up to.

Henry Francis Fynn

Henry Fynn was born in 1803 and trained as a surgeon's assistant in London, England. He moved to Cape Colony and learned the Xhosa language. After moving to Port Natal, he learned isiZulu and learned about Zulu culture by living with Shaka and his people. Fynn's diaries and sketches are important records about the Zulu leader and Nguni history.

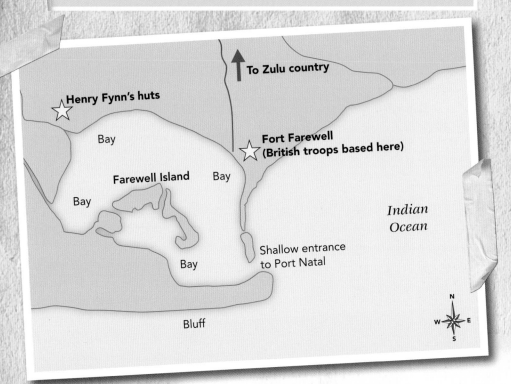

The British could load and unload goods from their ships in the sheltered waters of Port Natal. But they were under the watchful eyes of the Zulus.

We have been trading ivory and skins with the British for metals and fine cloths. As their traders have got richer, more settlers have arrived to get rich, too. Everything is peaceful between our people, but who knows what the future holds?

Watching us

Fynn is fascinated by me and my people. He spends hours watching women and children farming, men sharpening their spears, and all kinds of things that happen every day. He writes and draws in books of paper. He looks shocked when I order cowardly soldiers or other people I do not trust to be killed under the killing bush at KwaBulawayo. He thinks I am cruel, but it is only my Zulu way.

"On a mere sign by Shaka ...the pointing of his finger, the victim would be seized by his nearest neighbors; his neck would be twisted and his head and body beaten with sticks."

Henry Fynn, 1824–1836

My people are terrified of me as they would be of a powerful god. They will kill on my command and are powerless to refuse me.

Death of Nandi

My saddest day has come; my mother, Nandi, died last week. But why are my people not as sad as I am? I feel like killing those who do not wail or cry like me, even women about to be mothers themselves. I would be nothing without Nandi, and no mother will ever be as great. I will order no crops to be planted this year. Cattle will be killed and no milk will be drunk. My people's lives should fall apart as mine has.

Nandi's tomb was a grain pit. Her servants were killed and buried alongside her, like any important Zulu.

Document it!

Shaka's grief made him angry and more ruthless than ever. Any death in a family causes confusion and sadness, but it is also an occasion to celebrate someone's life. You can remember your loved ones in your journal. Add photos, create a family tree, and make a timeline of their history, too.

Tensions rising

Tensions are rising among the Zulus. In 1828, I sent my army south to capture territory near Cape Colony, so that we could trade with the British there. When they returned, I sent them immediately to fight in the north. Why not? Zulu warriors can take continuous warfare. My aunt and my brother Dingane say nothing, but I have seen them exchange looks. Do they question my leadership?

"I need no bodyguard at all, for even the bravest men who approach me get weak at the knees and their hearts turn to water...They know no other will except that of their King, who is something above, and below, this earth."

Shaka

There is something I do not trust about Dingane, even though he is my brother.

After Shaka

On September 22, 1828, Shaka was murdered. His bodyguard and half-brothers Dingane and Mhlangana stabbed him near his military barracks at Dukuza. As an insult, they left his body in the open for hyenas to eat. But people loyal to Shaka buried his body in a grain pit in the Royal Herd pen.

> *"Hey brother! You kill me, thinking you will rule, but the swallows will do that."*
>
> (By "the swallows," Shaka meant the white people, because they made their houses of mud, as swallows do.)

The Voortrekkers

Voortrekkers were farmers of Dutch origin who escaped the harsh rule of the British at Cape Colony in search of a new life. From the 1830s onward, they spread outward through tribal lands, many of which were empty after the Mfecane.

The Voortrekkers arrived by land in the Zulu kingdom after their trip in wagons from the Cape. This was the Great Trek. They proved a formidable fighting force against the Zulus.

These modern Zulu people are enjoying a barbecue. Their lives are mostly very different than those of people in Shaka's time.

New leader

Shaka had no children, so Dingane became leader of the Zulu nation—but only after executing Mhlangana and his other brothers. Within two years of Shaka's death, the Voortrekkers had arrived in Zulu lands from Cape Colony. This started the first wars between Zulus and white people.

Changes to Zulu land

From the 1840s, the British gradually took control of southern Africa from the Voortrekkers and other settlers, especially after large amounts of valuable gold and diamonds were found in the territory in the 1860s. In 1879, the British army attacked the Zulus, since they were a threat to British settlers. Shaka's kingdom was broken up and became part of the state of South Africa, ruled at first by the British and more recently by an elected government. Today, the state of KwaZulu-Natal is homeland to the Zulu people who are descendants of Shaka's time.

Timeline

1787 Shaka is born to Nandi and Senzangakona

1793 Nandi and Shaka go to live with the Langeni

1802 Nandi and Shaka leave the Langeni during a drought and join the Mthethwa

1809 Dingiswayo becomes leader of the Mthethwa

1810 Shaka becomes a soldier in Dingiswayo's army

1816 Senzangakona dies; after defeating his brother, Shaka becomes chief of the Zulus; he builds his kraal at KwaBulawayo

1817 Mfecane begins

1818 Death of Dingiswayo; Shaka defeats Zwide and his Ndwandwe forces at the Battle of Gqokli Hill

1822 Mzilikazi defects from Shaka and leads the Ndebele people from the region

1824 HMS *Antelope* is the first British ship to arrive at Port Natal (present-day Durban); after Fynn saves his life, Shaka grants him possession of land at the port

1827 Nandi dies, and the country is forced to go into mourning

1828 Shaka sends his warriors to the borders of Cape Colony and then north of Zulu lands

1828	Shaka is killed by his half-brothers Dingane and Mhlangana on September 22
1835	Great Trek: Boers leave Cape Colony and occupy new areas of southern Africa
1838	Dingane murders Piet Retief and other Voortrekkers; Dingane and his forces are defeated by the Boers at the Battle of Blood River
1840	After a further defeat, Dingane flees to Swaziland, where he is killed; Mpande becomes Zulu ruler
1852	British take control of Cape Town
1867	Large diamond deposits are discovered at Kimberley, and the British decide to bring the country into the British Empire
1879	The Zulu army, led by Cetshwayo, defeats the British at Isandlwana, but it is later defeated at Ulundi, Natal
1880– 1881	Anglo-Boer War: The Boers rebel against the British, leading to battles between the British army and Voortrekkers and other people of Dutch ancestry in South Africa
1899– 1902	Boer War between British and Boers; the British win
1910	South Africa is born as a union of British- and Boer-dominated states

Fact File

Rulers after Shaka

Dingane Under Dingane, the Zulus got into conflicts with the British at Port Natal and with the Voortrekkers. In 1838, he executed over 100 Voortrekkers and then attacked their camps, killing 500. The Voortrekkers regrouped and avenged their comrades at the famous Battle of Blood River. Their force of 460 with guns defeated 10,000 Zulus with spears, killing 3,000. Dingane burned his kraal and fled. Dingane's half-brother Mpande joined the Voortrekkers and helped them defeat Dingane. He was then installed as Zulu king.

Cetshwayo Cetshwayo was the son of Mpande, who revived the Zulu army after Mpande's death in 1872. In 1878, diamonds were discovered in other areas of South Africa, and the British decided to take over the country. They invaded Zululand and, although Cetshwayo beat the British several times, the Zulus could not withstand the superior weapons of the British and were defeated. Cetshwayo was captured and sent to London, England, where he met England's Queen Victoria. He was restored to his throne, and Zululand became one of 13 chiefdoms established by the British. He died in 1882.

Zulus in the 20th century

Zulus were involved in the conflict known as the Boer War from 1899 to 1902, working for both the British and the Boers—for example, as trench diggers. In 1910, after the British had won the war, Zululand became part of the Republic of South Africa. In the 1948 elections, the National Party won and started the policy of apartheid. This meant that black people and mixed-race people in the country lost many rights. For example, they could not marry white people, use the same public transportation as white people, or live outside areas of the country called homelands, including kwaZulu. Apartheid did not end until 1990. Following democratic elections in 1994, Nelson Mandela became the first black president of the country. KwaZulu then became the state of kwaZulu-Natal.

Write Your Own Journal

What sort of journal would you make to record events from your life? Would it mostly be words, or would you illustrate it with sketches and photos? Would you include newspaper clippings, plane tickets, or anything else that will help you to remember important, happy, or special events? There are two main ways you can create a journal.

On paper

Some journals are created on paper. First, decide how big you want your journal to be. You can buy bound notebooks or scrapbooks of different sizes. But you can also make your own from folded large sheets of paper with thicker cardboard on the outside. Bind the spine using ribbon or string pushed through holes made with a hole punch.

You could also use a three-hole folder with loose, punched sheets of paper put in. The advantage of this is that you can add more pages as you create the journal and also different types of pages. For example, there may be plain pages for sketches, envelopes containing tickets, programs, or other souvenirs, as well as lined pages for neat handwriting.

On-screen

Other journals are created on a computer. There are several advantages of on-screen journals over paper ones. For example, you can type in and edit what you have written, scan in photos, load digital images onto pages, and easily shift images around and change their sizes. You can also make identical copies of what you have made to give to friends or family. However, you may not always be near a computer to keep this sort of journal up-to-date, and if there is a power outage or you forget to save, your precious memories could become unavailable or even lost!

Glossary

amabutho regiment of warriors in Zulu army divided from others by age

apartheid law in South Africa from 1948 to 1990 under which black people were forced to live separately from white people and suffered a variety of inequalities

barracks set of buildings where soldiers live

bull's horns strategy fighting strategy developed by Shaka in which groups of soldiers move around the enemy in a shape that resembles a bull's head and horns

Cape Colony area around what is now Cape Town settled by Dutch people in the early 17th century and taken over by the British in the early 19th century

chiefdom group of families led by a chief who normally inherits the role from his father

clan group of families of the same ethnic background

context circumstances and setting that help to make an action, idea, statement, or event easier to understand. For example, Shaka punished the Langeni people in the context of their mistreatment of him and his mother when he was young.

Dingiswayo leader of the Mthethwa chiefdom

grain pit hole for storing dry grain for use later. Grain pits were also used as burial sites by the Zulus.

heir person entitled to the property or the position of someone who has died

hunter-gatherer person who moves around a region to hunt or forage foods from the wild rather than farming in a fixed location

immigrate permanently move to live in a foreign country or region

induna officer in the Zulu army

isiZulu language of the Zulu people

kraal area surrounded by an outer fence containing huts for a clan or larger group of people in southern Africa. There is an inner fenced area for cattle.

KwaBulawayo Shaka's first capital city

Langeni chiefdom of Nguni people who lived near the Zulus

Mfecane period of movement of chiefdoms and tribes in southern Africa, caused partly by aggression and expansion by the Zulu people

Mthethwa chiefdom of the Nguni tribe that Shaka's mother came from, and among whom Shaka lived from his teenage years

Nandi mother of Shaka

Nguni tribe of African people that originated in central Africa and moved southward in the first millennium BCE

Senzangakona father of Shaka and king of the Zulus until his death, when Shaka succeeded him

slave person legally owned by others, who is forced to obey and work for them. Many African slaves were taken by European people to do their hard work in mines, in fields where crops for sale were grown, and in their homes during the 18th and 19th centuries.

successor someone who takes over another person's role after the original person has gone or given it up

sugar plantation farm where sugarcane is grown as a crop, harvested, and processed into sugar. In the 17th century, this work was usually carried out by slave labor.

tribe group of people with culture, language, and political organization in common yet who do not necessarily all live in the same place or region

Voortrekker person of Dutch descent living in the Cape Colony in the 19th century, who moved northeast into other parts of southern Africa

Zulu stick fighting sport and martial art that is part of Zulu culture and, in the past, important as training for war. Two people compete, and each person has two sticks and a shield.

Zwide leader of the Nwandwe chiefdom, enemies of the Mthethwa people

Find Out More

Books

Cawthorne, Nigel. *Victory: 100 Great Military Commanders*. New York: Metro, 2012.

Nelson, Kadir. *Nelson Mandela*. New York: Katherine Tegen, 2013.

Throp, Claire. *South Africa* (Countries Around the World). Chicago: Heinemann Library, 2012.

Trejo, Aaron. *Zulu Warriors* (History's Greatest Warriors). Minneapolis: Bellwether Media, 2012.

Web sites

www.apartheidmuseum.org/comics
Read an online comic about life under apartheid at the Apartheid Museum web site.

www.english.emory.edu/Bahri/apart.html
Discover more about the apartheid laws and their impact on life for the majority of South Africans on this web site.

www.sahistory.org.za/people/king-shaka-zulu
This web site has short, informative biographies of different African leaders, including Shaka Zulu.

www.timeforkids.com/destination/south-africa/native-lingo
Want to hear some isiZulu language being spoken? Visit this web site to find out how to say basic phrases such as "hello," "goodbye," and "cool."

www.zulu-culture.co.za/index.php
Learn about all kinds of aspects of Zulu life, from crafts and dancing to food and religion.

Places to visit

Apartheid Museum
Corner of Northern Parkway and Gold Reef Roads
Ormonde, Johannesburg
South Africa
www.apartheidmuseum.org
If you ever get the chance to go to South Africa, you could
visit the Apartheid Museum. It has many photos, artifacts,
and displays about apartheid and the 20th-century history of
South Africa.

KwaZulu-Natal Museum
237 Jabu Ndlovu Street
Pietermaritzburg
South Africa
www.nmsa.org.za
The KwaZulu-Natal Museum has exhibitions on the history of
the state, from the earliest people and African and European
settlers to wildlife and Zulu culture.

The Metropolitan Museum of Art
1000 Fifth Avenue
New York, New York 10028-0198
www.metmuseum.org
The Metropolitan Museum of Art has an extensive collection of
African art, including many Zulu objects such as bowls, belts,
and drums.

Index